MUSE

ANGELYN GUMBS

Copyright @2021 by Angelyn Gumbs

All rights reserved. No part of this book may be reproduced in any form or by any electronic or mechanical means, including information storage and retrieval systems, without permission in writing from the publisher, except by reviewers, who may quote brief passages in a review.

This publication contains the opinions and ideas of its author. It is intended to provide helpful and informative material on the subjects addressed in the publication. The author and publisher specifically disclaim all responsibility for any liability, loss or risk, personal or otherwise, which is incurred as a consequence, directly or indirectly, of the use and application of any of the contents of this book.

WORKBOOK PRESS LLC
187 E Warm Springs Rd,
Suite B285, Las Vegas, NV 89119, USA

Website: https://workbookpress.com/
Hotline: 1-888-818-4856
Email: admin@workbookpress.com

Ordering Information:
Quantity sales. Special discounts are available on quantity purchases by corporations, associations, and others.
For details, contact the publisher at the address above.

ISBN-13:   978-1-954753-03-7 (Paperback Version)
            978-1-954753-04-4 (Digital Version)

REV. DATE: 09/02/2021

by,
Angelyn

"Black"

What a Strong and Beautiful Color.

"Oh yeah"!

It's also Sexy too.

Shy Girl,

Shy girl never smiles,
Shy girl,
Covers her eyes,
Shy girl,
Held head down low,
Shy girl,
Muffles her word so .
Shy girls,
Always surprise the world..

Autumn Colors ,

*Red, Yellow , Orange and Gold .
Search a beauty thy eyes behold.
It's warms the heart to sing,
Autumn Colors,
What a magnificent Joy it brings.*

"*Apologies* "

Apologies don't fit here anymore.
This is why ,
You must move from my door.

"Those things are a part of life."

The eeks!
"the Hums, hahaha and the oh no's."
Those things are just a part of life.
That's just the way it goes.

"Love can"

Love can be so amazing for all to see. You'll say bye -bye to loneliness and hello to mellow.
for the sunshine again.
you just have to be loved.
Love can take you on so many journeys and leave you so overjoyed with happiness.
love can have you flying to the moon and stars above.
Love can.

'God'

God puts mountains and hills for us to climb
"Life is a mountain that's worth the climb."

"Would you stay with me ?"

If I capture all the stars in the night sky, and lay them down at your feet.
If I fed you ambrosial throughout the years and time.
If I sing you a song in the moonlight by the Oceanside.
If I drop to my knees in daily devotional, asking to have you near me.
I'm determined to show you how much
I love you.
By all the tears of joy I have cried.

"Dreaming about you"

I have been dreaming about you,
So when I heard your voice yesterday,
I knew something beyond my dreams was heading my way.
Dreaming about you,
"My heart!"
Oh how it just can't stop skipping a beat.
I'd waited for so long for your love,
Dreaming about you,
Being with you is what I held on to for years.
Dreaming about you,
When I think about the way that you use to kiss me.

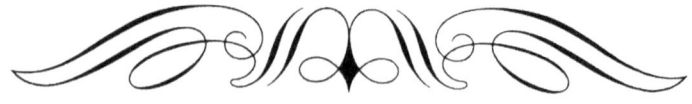

"It was magical!"
You took my Doubts, Fears and Anger away.
Dreaming about you,
" I am so wanting to run right back into your arms."
Right here and now!
"But you are, so ,so far away."
Dreaming about you,
I keep telling myself that in spite of it all .
My love for you, and yours for me.
Is standing alongside , with Romeo and Juliet's.
Our love has been a test of time.
Dreaming about you,
It has finally come true.

"Reset"

How amazing life would be if we all could press a reset button?
When things start going wrong,
"we just press and then we will continue along."
A do over on mistakes, misunderstandings, miss opportunities and misfortunes.
And of course on the one who got away.
That's a giving!
"Press reset on all those regrets."
A reset on life and on our relationship with God.
When we call out our Father's name, whether it's
Yahweh, Jehovah,
God or Allah.
When we press the reset button our Savior will answer our calls.

"Who would have thought?"

That love could show so much
strength and respect.
Damn!
"And could be funny too!"
Who would have thought?
That love would be put to the test and stand out above all
the rest.
Who would have thought?
That love could be everything and anything it should.
Who would have thought? That love could be true.
"I guess only love knew."

"A Christmas love"

That seems to go beyond heartbreak.
A Christmas love , that no words can't speak.
A Christmas love, that causes the heart and soul to grow.
So pass the measure of time. A Christmas love , so strong and so true.
Here's to A Christmas love ,
when it comes to me and you.

"Excuses"

To all the things you said and did wrong.
Excuses,
Always seem to follow along.
Excuses,
Couldn't hear the phone or get out of bed on time.
Excuses,
Is all that you gave me.
Excuses,
When it's all said and done, no more excuses.
"Because I am about to run !"

"On days like this"

just want to sit down and cry,
As the tears roll out my eyes.
On days like this, it's always why, why, why.
On days like this, don't care to see the parting of the clouds for the sun.
On days like this, the birds how they sing don't mean anything.
On days like this, not even a smile can take the darkness away.
On days like this.

"Tell Me"

*You're so boring,
that even your smile makes me yawn.
"Tell Me, shall I go on ?"*

"I Need"

I need to get to W, X, Y and Z.
To see what's waiting for me.
Is it love or is it just money,
just hoping that it wouldn't be disappointment there,
I know this wouldn't be funny.
Does anyone care ?

"Didn't Know"

Kiss could be so engaging with power.
Like thunder and yet soft and gentle like a flower.
Just to have the understanding,
that a kiss can bring the strongest men weak to their knees.
Look at the eyes ,how they water and cry.
Every time a kiss says goodbye.
Didn't know that the kiss has a heart, mind and soul .
For the kiss has always been in control.

"Passion !"

I bite my lips, as he works his way between my thighs.
Can't help but to beg for more,
My heart races as I take deep breaths.
"You know that feeling?"
When it feels so damn good.
Our bodies intertwine as the sweat runs down our spines.
We dance and twirl in the sheets,
As it comes to the finish !
I gave out my loudest and most passionate cry.
He gently moved closer and whispered into my ear.
"The pleasure was all mines.,"
To keep bringing you to your knees.
Because I am a man who pleases.

"*I understand*"

I understand why the rain falls,
I understand why the seasons change,
I understand the stars in the night sky.
I understand the color green,
I understand life and all the challenges it brings.
I understand the small and big things. But what
I don't understand, How do you stop loving me? Now that
I am He ?

"Bestfriend"

At times we'll hold hands,
Bestfriend,
No secret are kept to hide,
Bestfriend,
We'll laugh and we'll cry ,
Bestfriend,
I am yours and you are mine.

"No More Tears"

No more tears of sadness,
No more tears of fears,
No more tears of loneliness
Only tears of happiness.
If I could I would give you.
No more tears,

"A Smile"

What is it about a smile?
It can be shy at times,
also very sexy and sly.
Even mysterious too.
When it's not playing pretend with you.
A smile can always say Hi.
Oh yeah!
A beautifully smile can,
"say it all and do it all!"
So I will smile for you.

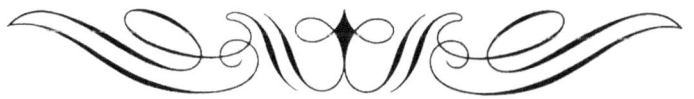

"Thank you Lord"

Even though the days and night had been hard.
We still remember to give you praise.
Thank you Lord,
For guiding us in our darkest times.
Thank you Lord,
You regain our strength to overcome each, and every obstacle.
That got in our way,
Thank you Lord,
Our faith is so strong.
As we smile and sing praises to you.
We say Amen,
Thank you Lord.

"Oh Look"

Oh Look what they have done to us.
They took us from our home lands, where we were once Kings and Queens.
Oh Look what they have done to us. Bond and chained us in the bottom of ships .
Not even cattle get treated like this,
They took our languages or names and our beliefs too.
Oh look what they done to us,
Told us that they God wasn't our God.
And it was his law to make us slaves.
Because they God saw us as the children and the people of the Devil.
Oh look what they have done to us,
They told us that our skin colors tones and our hair.
That some were of beauty ,
while others were just plain ugly.
So when we look at each other,
we don't see that we are all one family.
But jealousy and hatred,
Because the fair skin was better than the dark skin.

And curling and smooth hair was better,
than the dry natural hair, which they call nappy.
Oh look what they have done to us,
They started calling us Nigger, Negro and colored too.
They even call our Men boys.
Oh look what they have done to us,
We have lost our beauty and respect for each other and our families,
Which was once a great and large part of who we are.
Oh look what they have done to us,
We know that they are laughing, everytime that they hear us.
Using those same words of pain and disgust to each other.
Oh look what they make us into,
They saw us as slaves yesterday and still today.
Oh look what they teach us,
"About our history!"
Nothing really.
Because they have made us a shame.
Of who we are, and where we came from. Oh look how they only give us, one month to talk about our history.
And yet some of us are still afraid to open those books.

That opens the doors to our past.
So we just open it up just a little, for people like
Dr. Martin Luther Jr. etc. to pass through,
They refuse to let it go any farther.
In the schools and at home.
Oh look what they have made us,
To be ashamed to be Black, Africa and Carribean too.

"Grace"

I was once like a rabid dog with a bone.
But then Grace fell upon me.
Now I'm waiting to go home.

"Mirror"

*Why don't you show me ?
Can this really be ,
Me ?*

" *Snowflakes* "

On my eyelashes, snowflakes on my tongue.
Look how they fall to the ground.
Snowflakes all around.

"*Spoken Words*"

If words were served up on a silver platter.
If words couldn't shatter,
so strong and yet still so weak.
Full of beauty and full of pain.
Spoken Words not of anger.
But Spoken Words on a platter.

"Invisible Me"

Standing or sitting in the corner.
Invisible Me,
Don't anyone see,
A tree,
Everyone has to stop and look at,
a tree from the trunk to the branches.
"Even that green moss that grows screams look at me!"
Invisible Me,
The stars in the night sky.
See how bright they shine.
Invisible Me,
Flowers take a pick.
Invisible Me,
Nobody can see.
Invisible to the whole world.
Or just invisible to me?

"My Shoulders"

There are times when a pillow won't do.
Here's when I lend my shoulders to you.
So cry on my shoulders there here for you.
Just tilt your head to left or right .
As the tears fall ,
I know that I'll get a smile in the end.
My shoulders can be a pillow,
as I am a friend.
To lend them to you.

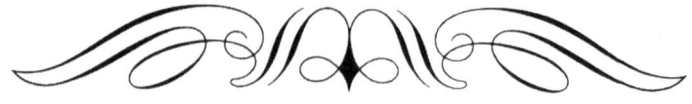

"The Cross He Carried"

So heavy that his back the pain was worth bearing.
He carried the Cross,
as his enemies were cheering.
For those who loved him was tearing. Carrying the cross
not with guilt or shame,
or other words of disgrace,
For placing a crown of thorns on his head.
The laughter as the blood sweat ran down his face. All
because he chose to die for all our Sins.
So our Sins are now forgiving.
Because he was placed on that cross that he carried.

"Let's"

Let's talk and lend a hand
Let's smile at everyone when we make eye contact.
Let's laugh out loud.
Let's spin round and round as we jump up and down.
Let's hold hands together.
Let's look away how we are not the same, and focus on how we are.
Let's light up the world with a song and dance.
Let's just make friends and not enemies.

"Haunted House"

"It was straight out of a Halloween story."
The color has been washed away with years and time.
Ghostly vines cover the doors frames.
Window sills with curtains of cobwebs, cracked and chip walls . That were once hung with paintings.
The ceiling is now covered with the age of stain.
Bats !
Swarm from room to room, up and down every hall.
Old candelabras with melted candle wax still in place.
Dust and soot lingers in the air while shadows sails across.
The rats and the mice danced on the keys of a baby grand.
That once played symphonies for galas.
The creaks and squeaks of the floors and the howling of the wind.
That's the only sound   you will hear, even though others have said to hear a moan or groan.
I will tell you that wasn't of the undead.
Can't help but to get chills when you think about who once lived there.

Behind that rusty iron gate in that house, was it pure with love or evil.
So when you stop and look at that old Victorian three story house. It's hard to see if it's just a fixer upper or something more.

"Eyes"

Eye's are not of lost
Eye's not only wholes search wonder from all around
Eye's not only filled with emptiness
Eye's so mysterious
Eye's can be seen like a lost treasure to be found Eye's are all around.

"Waiting for that star to fall"

In the midnight hour ,
I'm looking to the sky to see,
all my little and my big dreams.
For all those years,
I've waited for that star.
Therefore tonight wouldn't be a fantasy.
It's about to come true,
Just waiting for that star to fall.

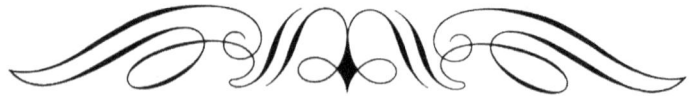

"The Hole"

You have fallen into a hole.
Struggling to get out,
cries for help are heard by the onlookers.
Looking and speaking out the words of strength, to help
lift you up.
the words seem to go on and on as they keep preaching.
To lend that hand.
But as you reach to grab a hold,
so you can get out of the hole
Here's the shocker , they never kept what they preach.
Saying tomorrow they will be there for you when you
need them today.
So here you are, in the hole again and again.

"Remember to sing"

Happy Birthday Dr. King.
Oh how he makes us want to sing,
For all the changes he had bring,
to all races and Creed.
That we had to follow.
Remember to sing
Happy Birthday Dr. King.
His speeches was
For the love for all and nonviolence.
Was the way to go.
For America was filled with so much shallowness among
all the races.
We have overcome with such Joy.
As we sing ,
Happy Birthday, Dr. Martin King

"A Month"

A month filled with so much pride,
A month to hold your head up high,
A month to wear your biggest smile ,
A month that was once only a dream,
But now it's real ,
For all those who came before us
Thank you ,
For given us our black pride ,

"God's eyes"

God's eyes are watching,
God's eyes are watching,
We all are hiding too afraid.
To let God in,
So we'll just open the door and show a little peep into the soul.
Hiding emptiness and anger inside.
Calling out when things are beyond our control.
That's when we yell out for a hand.

"Why Stay"

When all you have to do is runaway.
Easy for one to say,
When thought this was the one.
No idea, that eyes will be black and blue.
So covering them is what's left to do.
Those three words have no more meaning anymore.
As the years now roll down from the eyes
Being to walk out that door
You won't be able to hurt me anymore.

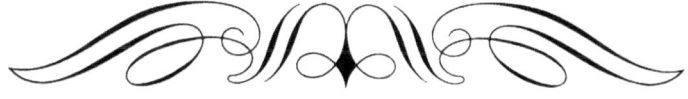

"Words"

Look at you and then look at me.
For we are much more than the words, that made us up to be.
But the gift that granted us with a soul. So now you see, that it's now all made complete.

"The thing about first Love"

Is that it can't hide,
even though it may attend to.
Filled up with so much hope that no one will see.
Upon wearing a disguise
It's like guess what?
Surprise!
"Yes,"
This I kid you not, this is true.
What I say is No lie.
When it comes to first love..
The one thing that it would never do.
That is Die.

"I can't believe"

*I can't believe that,
I am falling for Fall again.
Oh my goodness,
Winter is going to be so bitter cold.*

"Flatulence!"

We wish that we could live without it.
"Oh yeah!"
It says a lot by it smell,
what we ate for breakfast, lunch, dinner and dessert too.
No matter how old we get,
We still feel uncomfortable, and laughing at each other.
When it comes to that raspberry - AKA Fart!

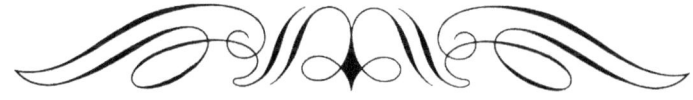

"Train of Life"

Standing in the station with so many byways,
folks from all around in and out.
handing over my four pieces of baggage that's tag h.w.c.
holding on to my ticket,
Line up!
"A loud voice over the intercom says" walking until seeing a spot.
standing in line can't see ahead.
it's like step today and wait,
can't fall asleep people behind cut ahead.
empty stomach and afraid,
turn has gone by.
begins to weep, then hearing a voice, saying hold on.

'Angels'

With such beauty of light.
That these Angels take flight.
Just are watching over us both day and night.
Voices of a choir of hymns,
with beauty and Psalm of David the Angels sings.
Bringing a joyful note to the Lord's face.
When the kingdom of the heavenly host host of ,
Angels take Their place.

Standing in the breeze,

Standing in the breeze.
Listening to birds and picking daisies.
As they sprout up beside the trees.
Ooh !
The grass had never looked so green. Just standing in the breeze,
when these things were noticed by me.

"What is it about me that scares you?"

Looking in the mirror,
I begin to wonder what I see ?
Is it my eyes ?
For they aren't blue, hazel or green,
but more of a deep dark brown.
What is it about me that scares you ?
Is it my nose?
For not being long thin and
pointed at the tip,
For mine is big and flat shaped, my nostrils are opened
wide on both sides. What is it about me that scares you ?
Is it my lips ?
For it doesn't look like an artist has drawn it onto my
face.
For it's not sleek or even too thin,
but my lips are full from my top lip to the bottom.
And as for these lips have ,never even hang when they
are full.
What is about me that scares you?
Is it my hair?

For it's not straight like a horse's mane, or even the natural colors,
Blonde, Burnett and Red.
Just look how they shine bright
as the sun.
For my hair is thick and
long and coarse,
but yet still as soft as a sheep's wool.
And it doesn't really blow in the wind.
For my natural color,
it's of the night sky.
What is it about me that scares you?
Looking at my facial features,
then I say.
"Is it my skin tone ?"
That sets off all the emotions of fear and hate ?
Why is it so hard for so many of them to just understand
?
That when the creator of all things bestowed all the beauty upon the Earth. That the Black Race was included too in Beauty, not to be Feared or even Hate..

"Tell me"

Why you're so boring, that even your smile makes me yawn.
Tell me,
"shall I go on ?"

"The Holidays"

Brings a warm and calm feeling.
The Holidays,
Yet it can have that lonely and emptiness too.
The Holidays,
Can be filled with so much
joy and happiness.
The Holidays,
It's what brings us together,
and yet apart.
So I say,
The Holidays days Is what you make it.

'Picture'

Can be revealing, also very much deceiving.
From this point of view.
Just seeing all the different ways,
that one has to overcome.
In order to see you.

"Jumping around."

*Right under the sky , as arms open wide.
Catching that Dinero, Pounds, Argent, Geld, that Money !
Before it hits the ground.*

"Today"

*I'm removing all the ifs in my life.
I have now found out,
"That the It's in life, are of power and strength."*

"Outer of my mind?"

Am I outer of my mind?
when looking at birds fly.
Am I outer of my mind?
when overcome by the words on the pages.
Am I outer of my mind?
lost in comical laughter.
Am I outer of my mind?
hiding from a world that's too hard to understand.
Am I outer of my mind?
when just seeing that they all have it planned.

Tired of Relationship.

*So tired of this bipolar relationship.
It's time to get off this merry go round.
and the Ferris wheel of up and down.
I'm kicking off my shoes, and saying
"to Hell with you."*

"As Children"

Learning the hymn, Jesus loves the little children, All the children of the world; Red and yellow black and white, They are precious in his sight;
It has been a good song for the four walls of churches On the outside those lyrics have not standed to be true. When one color has always been degrading all the others.

"Dr. Martin Luther King."

As Dr. King sings with us those old spiritual hymns.
All praise to God, from an end to all the sadness and pain.
For prayers for love to reign,
Just see what joy it will bring.
His speeches are so strong and true, nothing forced or borrowed.
To preach for love for all, and nonviolence was the call.
Thank you Dr. Martin Luther King.

Truly Amazing,

When looking into your eyes and falling for that smile.
Truly Amazing,
Just you watching all the things you do.
Truly Amazing,
How you made love to me,
I would feel it, all the way down to my toes.
Then all the positions that you had me in.
" Oh my head did spin."
Truly Amazing,
For you have always taken the initiative not to .
A Boy but to be a Man.
Truly Amazing,
Not walking out on your responsibility, Even when they seem to be wearing you down.
Truly Amazing,
That all the places that you have been and seen
Truly Amazing,
That you always took a piece of me.
Truly Amazing,

That you still kept your
first a secret love.
Which no one could ever understand.
"Oh Man !"
Truly Amazing,
It hurts that you are gone,
And now too remembering,
all those memories and secrets shared.
Truly Amazing,
I'm holding on, knowingly that only God can judge me.
When others do.
Truly Amazing,
That you my first love would be so much better in
Heaven….
Truly Amazing,
"That No one,
would be able take you and anything else away from
me…"
Once in Heaven we'll see.

I Pray For Everybody

I pray for Everybody,
The good, the bad,
The strong, the weak,
Even the very strangers I meet.
What more can I say?
We all just have to pray.

Black Voice,

*Strong and demanding,
Black Voice,
Can leave you laughing.
Black Voice,
You must raise your hands.
Black Voice,
At times it's hard to take a stand.
Black Voice,
But we all have to come to understand.
Black Voice, Black Voice, Black Voice!!*

Painted sky & Painted wall

*However the paint dries
the chips will fall.
"Oh yes,
That's where the drama comes to call.
Painted sky from blue to grey,
Who's to say?
When it all comes into play,
Painted sky & Painted wall.
And what a day for us all.*

Love ,Love ,Love .

Oh we all hear it in songs,
Love that makes the heart pitter patter and skips a beat.
What is it about love ?
That even our souls can't wait to speak.
Love can make one feel strong and then yet again weak.
Very soon love will have you thinking about, when you first met.
Oh love, when it's all about love.
Look and you will see.
Right outside your window or at your very own door.
And in other cases down the street.
Love, Love, Love,
It's me.

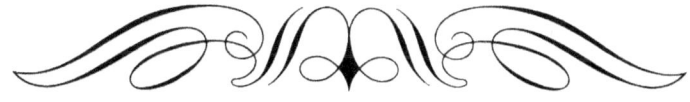

A Sexy Tango,

As you spin my body across the dance floor,
Lifting, grabbing as you stroking my inner thighs
A sexy Tango,
placing my breast along your chest,
A sexy Tango,
The rhythm of the beat lifts me off my feet.
A sexy Tango,
My hips do a slow and sexy whine, as our body grind
Now this is more, than a sexy Tango,
This is love bingo.

A Mother's Love ,

There's nothing that can compare to.
A Mother's Love ,
Is that Love that molds us into the people we are to be .
A Love that not only nurturing ,
But understanding as well,
A Mother's Love ,
Gives us the strength for this competitive world that we all seek.
A Mother's Loves ,
Not only fills our tummies but hearts ,
A Mother's Love ,
Is that love for the soul.

Free,

*As I close my eyes
And then sigh,
I'm free,*

He Loves Me,

In spite of my sins
in all
he loves me,
when the thunder calls
he loves me,
when the lightning flash
he loves me,
when the gentle and the strong wind blows
he loves me,
even when tears and rain falls
he loves me,
I know God loves me.
Even when I sinned he still hears my call.

I Can Fix That,

When the tears roll down your cheeks,
And it makes it hard for you to speak.
I can fix that.
When your world comes tumbling down,
I'll say it again.
For I can fix that,
By putting a smile on your face.
I'll take my time,
With the love we make
And I'll end it with a warm embrace
Just you start to believe,
That love is only a myth.
I can fix that,
With only a kiss.

Ladybugs,

Yellow and Red,
I ask you , where is my luck,
Or I'll squash you.

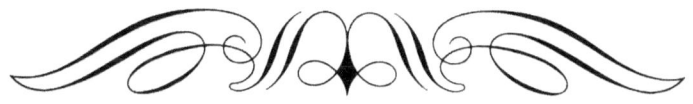

Everlasting Love,

*A Love that
stands out the test of time,
A Love that grabs a hold on your mind.
A Love that has no boundaries,
A Love that gives it's testimonies.
A Love that grows old.
A Love that can't be bought or sold,
So on our Wedding day I will release 50 white Doves.
To show the world our Everlasting Love.*

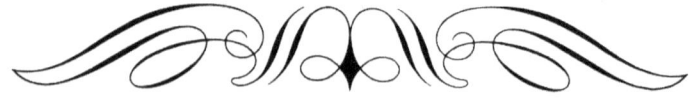

Heaven's Gate,

*I know Heaven gate will open wide just,
to welcome you inside.
I know all angels would gather around from miles .
Just to see that wonderful and warm smile.
Yes , I will miss you and cry everyday.
When anyone asked why am I crying?
I'll say these aren't tears of sadness but of joy.
For Heaven 's gate has open wide,*

Song,

*An incredible song, filled with harmonies of sweet
philein that captured me.
A melody for a clandestine,
Now that my heart and
should have a taste of philter,
I'm so in love with this so I'm going to hold on tighter
and tighter.
These lyrics have taken me
out of my own abyss.
This so incredible song from
the begin to the end,
Taught me love can always
come with a kiss.*

Baby,

*My baby giggles ,
when mommy tickles.
Now we both got the jiggles.*

Gems of the Earth

These precious stones that once covered the earth.
Carnelian, Chrysolite, Emerald, Topaz, Onyx and Jasper.
Handed them now the Holy Ghost,
Felt so strong and captivating.
The Gems of the Earth,
Has filled thy Heart and can't never depart.

Our Love

*Seeing how the wind blows,
with such a gentle breeze.
Now I know what your love means to me.
Fighting so hard to hold on to our happiness.
This love has already been pushed to the test.
From the very beginning,
to the end.
This love wasn't meant to stand hold on earth.
But to dance among the stars in heaven.
And there you'll be waiting with your arms wide open.
As I'm running straight to you.
Now this is how I love you.*

www.ingramcontent.com/pod-product-compliance
Lightning Source LLC
Chambersburg PA
CBHW071507070526
44578CB00001B/473